Rocks, Pebbles and Paint

This edition published in 2018
By **SpiceBox™**
12171 Horseshoe Way,
Richmond, BC,
Canada V7A 4V4

First published in 2011
Copyright © SpiceBox™ 2011

ISBN 10: 1-927010-12-8
ISBN 13: 978-1-927010-12-9

CEO and Publisher: Ben Lotfi
Artist: Danny Han-Lin Chen and Hilda Yuet Yi Chen
Editorial: Trisha Pope
Creative Director: Garett Chan
Art Director: Christine Covert
Design, Photography & Illustration: Charmaine Muzyka
Production: James Badger, Mell D'Clute
Sourcing: Janny Lam, Carman Fung

Special thanks to Tri-Art Acrylics Mft. (www.tri-art.ca) for sponsoring
the professional acrylic paints used on the projects in this book.

For more SpiceBox products and information, visit our website:
www.spiceboxbooks.com

Manufactured in China

9 10

Contents

Projects

Introduction

Rock painting is a fun, easy craft to do that everyone can enjoy. From the hunt for the perfect pebble, to the satisfaction of finding it, from painting the first layers of paint on the stone, to seeing your rock turn in to a frog, a butterfly, or even a puppy, rock painting is an enormously satisfying craft. You can use your own power of creation to transform the ordinary into the extraordinary of imagination.

Once you start, you will become hooked, so be prepared to never look at a rock in the same way again!

Wahoo!
We can't wait to see what you are going to create! Let's get started...

Let's get started!

In this book, we are going to show you how to find an ordinary rock, and turn it into something fantastic. You will be able to explore your artistic skills, as well as your creative vision. Painting on rocks is easy and fun, and with a few basic techniques you will be able to turn a pebble into a little bug, or find a rock that you can create a beautiful swan with.

Careful with the brush... I'm so ticklish!

Materials
some things you will need to work with

rocks

We will talk more about finding the perfect rocks later. However, in order to do rock painting, you will definitely need rocks!

gesso

Gesso is a kind of special white paint that you can use to cover the rock before you start painting. If you paint a layer of gesso on your rock, it will seal the rock and create a good base for painting with acrylics. The colors will be brighter, and you will use less paint for your design. You can paint directly onto your rock without adding a coat of gesso first, but you will likely need to use 2 or 3 coats of paint to achieve a nice color and finished design. It is easily purchased at any craft or art supply store, and is relatively inexpensive. You certainly can start painting without it though, and pick it up at a later date.

paints

The nicest paints to use are acrylic paints. Acrylic paint is bright and comes in lots of great colors. It is permanent and water resistant, which makes it ideal for painting on rocks. If you find your paint is too thick to get into all the crevices in the rocks, you can thin it with water to make applying it a bit easier.

Be sure to wear something to cover your clothes before painting, and wash any splatters immediately, before they dry.

brushes

You will want to use a few different sizes of brushes as you get started. A wide, flat one will be good for painting large areas of your rock quickly. Small brushes in different sizes will be needed to paint the details of your creations and outline your designs.

Aside from brushes, there are many other things you may find around your house that will create fun textures and patterns on your rocks.

Try:

Toothpicks	Feathers
Cotton swabs	Drinking straw
Toothbrush	Sponge
Comb	

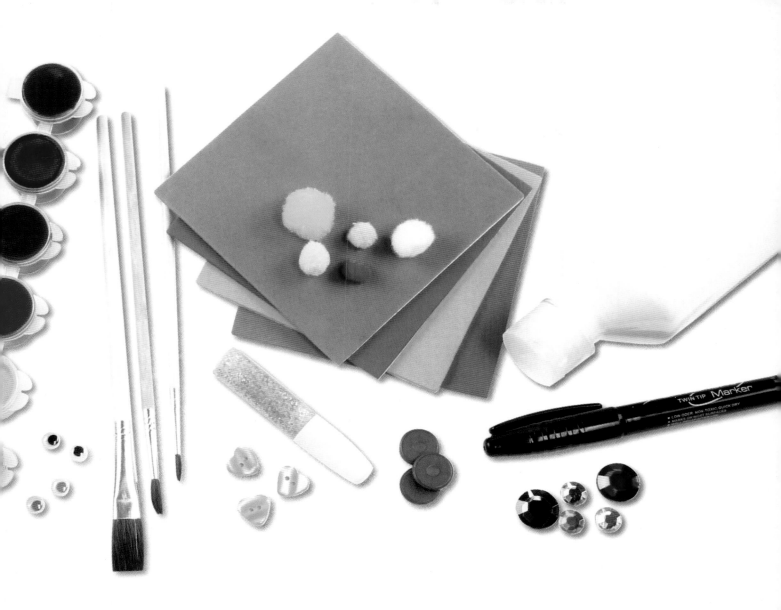

black marker

A black marker is useful for outlining the pattern on your rock. Try a few different felt tips to get the thickness you want, but a regular tip and a fine tip pen are a good place to start.

craft supplies

You can use lots of craft supplies to make your painted rock creations even more exciting. You can use felt pieces for feet, wings or a beak. You can add googly eyes or pipe cleaners, feathers and even glitter.

varnish & acrylic gel

Once you have painted your rock, you will need to protect the paint from chipping or rubbing off. The best way to do this is to coat your rock with a varnish or acrylic gel. A water-based, spray varnish that is used for furniture is easy to use and will protect your rock well.

Acrylic gel is a medium artists use to mix with their paint. It is also can be used to seal the paint onto your rock and can even be used as a glue. It is quite strong and will be more durable than a varnish. In either case, put on two layers of sealant to get the best protection for your rock art.

Choosing your rock

HINT: *After you clean your rock, write on the back in pencil what you want to paint on it. If you gathered lots of rocks, you may forget what they are supposed to be!*

The most fun part of rock painting can be exploring outside to find rocks that inspire your imagination. Rocks come in all shapes, sizes and colors and when you are choosing a rock you should take a few different things into consideration to help you pick just the right one.

One thing to know, is that you will not be able to paint on rocks that have been polished - the shiny surface will not allow the paint to cling to it. Make sure you find your rocks in nature - the way they are made!

Color

Sometimes you may want to use the natural color of the rock to make the finished design more beautiful or lifelike. For example, if you are going to paint something light-colored like a rabbit or a swan, try to find a rock that is as light as possible. If you are going to paint a black bear, find a dark-colored rock. That way, if you have some of the rock showing through your painting, it will look natural and part of the piece.

If you are not planning to use the natural colour of the rocks, you can pick any color of rock, and then cover it with a gesso base coat to prepare the surface for painting.

size

Of course you can paint anything in any size, but you will probably feel more comfortable painting on a rock that you can hold in the palm of your hand, until you are more experienced. Teeny rocks are cute for turning into bugs and need a steady hand. Large rocks need a lot of paint and are harder to handle because they are heavy. If you are going to make the rock into magnet, choose a thin, light rock with a flat surface to glue a magnet to. Bigger rocks can become animals, dinosaur heads, or cars.

shape

This book features two styles of rock painting; two dimensional, where we paint an image on the surface of the rock, or three dimensional, meaning that we turn the entire rock into an object.

2D paintings use the rock as the painting surface. So, make sure you pick a rock with a nice surface for painting, and one that is large enough to accommodate your painting.

3D painting is the most creative and rewarding when it comes to looking for rocks. Each rock that you pick up can inspire your imagination to discover the perfect object to turn it into. Seeing images in a rock is a lot like staring at the clouds and imaging you see animals and faces in them. You can look at a rock that is bumpy and knobby, or broken in a certain way, or long and narrow, and see an object that comes to life as you paint it. As you pick up each unique and oddly shaped rock, try to imagine in your head what it could become.

2D rock painting

The picture is painted using the rock as the canvas.

3D rock painting

The entire rock is turned into a clever work of art — in this case, a scary dinosaur!

wash

dry

CAUTION!

It is important to keep your stones and pebbles in a safe place where your younger siblings cannot reach them and put them in their mouths. Please keep them in a storage container and placed out of the reach of young children!

Hints and Tricks

some handy pointers to get you ready:

Once you have selected your rocks, wash them well in warm soapy water. Rinse them off and let them dry on a paper towel, newspaper or rag that your parents don't need.

Prepare your work area by making sure it is well-protected. The rocks can get slippery when they are covered with paint, so you may accidentally drop them while you are painting. Make sure the table surface is protected by spreading the table with newspaper.

protect your
work surface

wear an old t-shirt

don't worry about your hands, everything washes off easily with soap and water

HINT: In art and craft stores, you can buy a large range of special acrylic paints that give lots of cool effects. You can buy glitter paint, metallic paints, and even glow-in-the dark paints to create amazing effects on your rock projects.

creating a practice drawing

Roughly trace the shape of your rock onto a paper. Use this paper drawing to determine how you are going to paint your picture on to the rock. This is especially helpful with more complicated paintings. When you have more practice, you can draw right onto your rock with a pencil. If you make a mistake you can cover it up with a layer of paint!

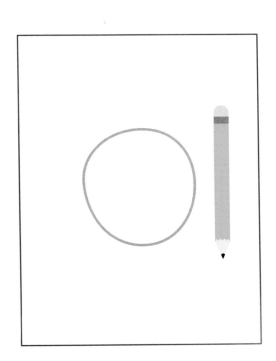

Painting Your Rocks

working with acrylic paint

• Brace your rock to keep it steady while it is drying. You can do this by crumpling up small pieces of paper and propping your rock up with them. Little pieces of plasticine also work really well, as does aluminum foil.

• As previously mentioned, you may want to paint your rock with gesso first so that your final painting is brighter. You can also mix a bit of your base color into the gesso to create a colored first coat if you would like that color to show through. If you want the rock color to show through, then you do not need to use the gesso.

• If you want, you can also use a coat of white acrylic paint. You will use up more of your paint if you use it as the base coat, but it will make the final results more attractive if you do not have gesso.

• If the paint gets on your clothing, clean it immediately with warm water and it should come off fairly easily. However, it is best to wear a painting smock, or clothes that you can get stained without your parents becoming angry!

• Wash your brush with warm water after you have finished painting or if you will not be using the brush for more than a few minutes. Acrylic is a permanent paint, which means that once it is dry, it will become hard it won't dissolve in water anymore. If you accidentally allow the paint to dry on your brush or clothes, it won't wash off with water, and you will need to buy a special acrylic cleaning solvent from a craft store to clean them. Fortunately, if you get acrylic paint on your hands it can be cleaned with warm water and soap even after it is dry.

Mixing Color

Let's review some basic color-mixing principles to help you create your own fabulous colors to paint with.

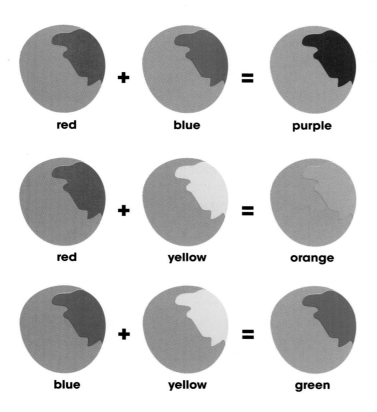

red + blue = purple

red + yellow = orange

blue + yellow = green

HINT: Be careful to keep your unvarnished rocks from rubbing together or from being dropped. The paint will chip and come off unless they are varnished.

Let's look back!

Did you know rock painting is so much fun, that people have been doing it for over 40,000 years? Different areas in Australia have been discovered by archeologists which show that people used "ochre" (a yellow-brown earth pigment) to create colored pictures on rock cave walls up to even 60,000 years ago!

It isn't very likely you will have ochre to paint your rocks with; acrylic is probably a better choice. However, you can use acrylic to mix all sorts of great colors. Try mixing a yellow-brown color to mimic ochre and create your own prehistoric rock art.

Gluing Your Rocks

Although many of the projects in this book are designed to be painted on a single rock, there is no limit to how you can combine rocks to make fantastic stone creations! Here are some basic tips on gluing rocks together, or adding on embellishments.

white craft glue:

You likely have white school glue around your home, and it will work. It dries quickly, but a disadvantage is that it doesn't dry clear and isn't the strongest glue. It will certainly work if you handle your rocks carefully after they are dry.

tacky craft glue:

There are extra strong white glues available in craft shops that are used in all sorts of crafting projects. This is a great type of glue to use as it bonds quickly and is fairly strong. It dries white, so you will need to cover it with paint or a decoration if you don't want it to show.

acrylic gel:

If you are able to find this, it is an excellent way to glue your rocks together because it is very strong. It also dries clear and also makes a good protective coating for your rock after you paint it. The only disadvantage is that it will take up to two days to dry completely.

bracing your rock while drying:

While you are waiting for your rocks to dry, you will need to brace them or prop them into the correct position so that they dry in the shape you want them to.

Paper or aluminum foil: Twist up bits of paper or foil, and use these to brace your rocks into position.

Plasticine or modelling clay: If you have this at home, you can make a molded shape to support your rock creations while they are drying.

Tape: Prepare masking tape by pressing it on your shirt or jeans and peel it off quickly a few times to remove some of the tackiness. Then wrap it around the pieces you are gluing to hold them into place while they dry. Do not use it on pieces that have already been painted as the tape may peel the paint off. Use this method only on unpainted rocks.

DRYING TIMES:

If you use a tacky craft glue, or a white glue, you will need the following time to allow things to dry:

Gluing rocks together: 3-4 hours in a sunny dry spot
Gluing fuzzy embellishments onto a rock: 2-3 hours
Gluing magnets or gemstones onto a rock: 2-3 hours

Pebble Babies

Pebble babies are so cute and simple to make! Find lots of tiny round rocks and make all kinds of little animals, just use your imagination! Place these in a plant pot in your home for a really cute decoration or on your window sill to brighten up your room.

Projects

Message Pebbles

wish rocks

Wish rocks are a wonderful project to start with. They are simple to make and fun to carry around in your pocket and share with friends! What would you like to wish for your friends: courage, happiness or luck? Paint it on a rock and give it to your best pal so they will remember you are always thinking of them.

1 Select small pebbles that have been worn smooth and feel nice in the palm of your hand. Wash them and paint them with gesso if you wish. Make sure they are dry before continuing.

2 Select a base color and cover one side of the rock. Let it dry. Flip the rock over and paint the rest in the same color. Let it dry.

TIP: Depending on the color of your rock, or if you painted it with gesso first, you may need to paint 2 or 3 coats of color to get a nice thick, bright base.

3 Lightly draw the word you have chosen onto your rock with a pencil. Carefully paint over it with a thin liner brush, or with a narrow flat brush, depending on the look you want.

4 If you wish, you can add embellishments like glitter or gem stones. Once your rock is dry, spray it carefully with varnish, or paint over it again with an acrylic gel to seal it. This will create a lovely, smooth surface that is shiny. It is perfect for rubbing when you need a bit of luck!

Anything you do is worth doing well, so keep this stone in your pocket to help you remember to give everything you do your best effort!

The next time your friend isn't feeling well, cheer them up by giving them this positive stone to hold as they concentrate on getting better.

Do you have a crush on someone? Keep this stone with you to help you focus those positive feelings towards that special person!

Chinese Symbols

Chinese symbols are exotic and also hold a lot of luck for many people. Here are some popular words you can use:

Peace

Love

Joy

Happiness

Kindness

fortune Telling Stones

Do you ever have a tough time making decisions or wonder what the result of your decision will be? Why not make a set of rocks that have all sorts of possible outcomes and advice. Follow the same steps as you did for the wish rocks, to create a selection of "Fortune Telling" rocks. Select small pebbles and paint them each with a different word or phrase:

- maybe later
- yes
- no
- It's love!
- ask an adult
- sure!
- are you crazy?
- never!

Keep your rocks in a tiny pouch, and when you have a difficult choice to make, consult your lucky stones!

Fridge Magnets

eggs

milk

cookies

Fridge Magnet Basics

Make a wonderful selection of magnets for your fridge, your locker, or a mirror frame in your room. Pick tiny rocks that will not be too heavy for the magnet you are using. These are equally cute whether you paint 2D images on them, or turn them into bugs, flowers, veggies and fruit or more!

Here we show you how to prepare your rocks for painting.
Follow these steps for all your rock magnets:

1 Gather a selection of small pebbles and rocks that are light and have a smooth place to glue a magnet to.

2 Clean your pebbles and let them dry. Once they are dry, trace around them on a piece of paper. Sketch your ideas onto the shapes you drew, to help you see how you want to position your design. Make sure you leave room to glue the magnet onto the back.

3 After they are cleaned and dried, paint any with gesso that you wish to and let dry.

4 Use a pencil to lightly transfer the design onto the rock. Don't forget you can paint over any mistakes!
Now you are ready to start painting your stones.

Ladybug Magnet

This ladybug is a charming insect to have on your fridge. Ladybugs bring good luck!

1 Make sure the base coat of gesso is completely dry. Then paint your pebble with a coat of red. Make sure you cover the entire rock completely.

2 With a pencil, lightly draw in the wings of the ladybug, and the face area. Use black paint and a fine brush to paint in the body and face.

TIP: To make the dots on the wings, you can paint them in freehand, or try "stamping" them on. You can use a toothpick, a cotton bud, or the eraser end of your pencil dipped in paint. Experiment with different ways to create dots on your paper first, and then choose the results you like the best.

3 When the black paint is completely dry, add the eyes in the same way as you added the black dots. A pencil eraser works well for larger dots. Use a toothpick to add in the mouth and the pupils of the eyes. A fine tip brush was used to paint in the antennae.

4 Once everything is completely dry, and you are happy with your bug, use tacky craft glue to glue the magnet on to the bottom of the pebble. You should also coat your entire rock in acrylic gel to protect it and give it a nice shine.

Flower Power!

These charming flower pebbles are simple to make. Pick bold, bright colors and paint in the background. Draw in your flower shapes, and paint them in with a fine brush.

Pumpkin Pebble

Create lots of these pumpkin pebbles and use them to decorate your table at Halloween! Paint the pumpkin orange, add in the stripes with a lighter orange or yellow, and then paint a funny or scary face.

Patterns

These pretty patterns are fun to paint freehand. Start with a small design in the middle of the pebble, and build your pattern out from there adding layers and color. Stop when you are pleased with the results!

Characters

These cute magnets can be made by copying the designs on the previous page, or use your imagination and paint on your own favorite animals! Paint a nice, thick base coat first, and let it dry thoroughly before adding your design. A fine-tipped black marker makes outlining easy.

Farmyard Fun

moo

oink oink

sheep

If mom and dad won't let you have your own horse, don't worry — you can make your own. And a pig, and a sheep, and a dog! Farm animals are a lot of fun to make, and when you are done you can build a little barn out of craft sticks for them to live in.

You will need:

- a large white pompom for the body
- medium rock for the head - painted white or left natural
- 2 x extra small rocks for the ears - painted black
- 4 x small rocks for the feet - painted black
- 2 x googly eyes
- masking tape
- craft glue

1 Once you have painted the ears and they have dried, glue them onto the head using a strong craft glue. Also glue on the eyes. You can use masking tape to hold the pieces in place until they dry. If the masking tape is too big, try tearing the pieces in half lengthwise to make skinnier strips of tape.

2 You will need to tape the feet to the pompom body with a piece of tape you have prepared. To prepare the tape, tear off a long piece, and, carefully holding each end, press the tape onto your shirt or pants once, and pull off quickly. This will make the tape a bit less sticky, so that it won't tear the pompom.

3 Dot glue on each foot and attach the front right foot and the back left foot. Secure them into place with a piece of prepared tape that is long enough to wrap around the body and both feet, holding them into place.

4 Glue on the front left foot and the back right foot in the same way; the tape will make an "x" across the body of the sheep.

5 Allow the glue to dry for 3 hours before you remove the masking tape.

6 Apply a generous amount of glue to the pompom where you want to attach the head. Apply glue to the back of the rock. Use masking tape to tape the head onto the body, wrapping the tape all the way around. Use a toothpick to dot even more glue where the head is connected to the body.

7 Allow the glue to set for 3-4 hours and then remove all the masking tape.

Chicken

1 This bean-shaped stone is perfect for making a chicken! Start by cleaning and painting the stone with gesso that has been mixed with yellow, to create a nice base color for the bird. Let it dry completely.

2 Use a bright orange to paint the body of the chicken, but let some of the yellow base color to show through, to create the look of feathers. Use a dark orange on the tummy of the chicken for shading.

3 The wings were painted with a very light yellow, and we added dark orange and white to create the look of feathers.

4 A yellow felt beak and googly eyes were glued on with a dot of craft glue, and then taped into place until they dried completely.

5 After the glue has dried, remove the masking tape. Cover the entire chicken with a coat of acrylic gel to give a shiny finish, and to protect it from damage.

Pig

Mix a light pink color for the body of your pig, and paint your rock completely with this color. Glue on eyes and a button nose, along with two pieces of pink felt or tiny pebbles painted pink for ears. Use masking tape to secure the pieces into place. If you have a small piece of pink yarn, you can also glue on a tail.

Horse

Find two oval rocks — one large and one small. If you want to add feet, find 4 very small pebbles as well. Paint the nose onto the head of the horse, and glue on eyes. Glue the head onto the body, using a generous amount of tacky glue. Tape the rocks together with masking tape to secure them, and add a bit more glue where the rocks are joined. Wait for 3 hours until the glue has dried.

Cut small pieces of yarn for the mane, and glue them onto the head and neck of the horse. Cut two small felt ears and glue them on each side of the head. Tape the pieces into place with a piece of tape prepared the same way you did for the sheep. Glue on the feet, if using, and tape them securely until the glue has dried.

Wait another 3 to 4 hours for everything to dry, and remove all of the masking tape.

Here are some other versions of farmyard friends. Find chunky rocks to create these cute cows and chicken, or be inspired by the shape of the rocks to paint other animals. Look at the gallery of rocks at the back of the book to inspire you!

Wild Animals Rock!

Leo the Lion

There is no doubt that many of the rocks you find will inspire you to create enough animals to fill a zoo! The shape of the rocks will help you imagine what animal is lurking inside. Use some of our examples to help get you started!

1 To paint Leo the Lion, start with a clean round rock, and give it a coat of gesso or white paint.

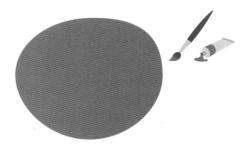

2 Add a base color that you think best suits your lion. We used a dark orange.

3 Use some of your base color to mix with white and create a lighter shade. (Don't use all of your darker color though, you will need it again!) Paint in the face shape.

4 Darken your mix with a bit of black or some of the darker color, and paint in the mouth area.

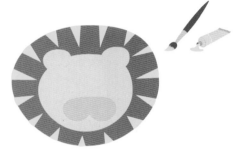

5 We used yellow to paint in the lion's mane detail.

6 Use your darkest color again to paint in the nose and ears.

7 Add some quirky eyes. You can either glue on googly eyes (here we used two different sizes) or you can paint them in.

8 Use white and black to add in shadow and highlights. Once you are pleased with the results, let your lion dry thoroughly, and use acrylic gel or a spray varnish to protect it.

Jenny Giraffe

Here we used the stone to create a 2D painting of Jenny Giraffe. Find a stone that is long and narrow to inspire you as a giraffe's neck will suit this shape!

1 Clean and paint your stone with gesso or a white acrylic base coat.

2 Mix white paint into your blue to achieve a light, sky blue color. Paint your stone with an even coat of this blue.

3 Practice drawing your design on a piece of paper. When you are confident, transfer your design to your stone with light pencil marks.

4 Once you have drawn on your design, select a base color for your giraffe (here we use yellow) and paint in the shape of the giraffe.

5 Use peach to paint in the nose. You can mix this color with a touch of red and yellow in white. You only need a bit, so don't mix too much!

6 The circles on the giraffe, as well as the inner ear are painted using a brown, lightened up with white.

7 Details should be added with a very fine brush, and black, brown and white paints.

8 Finally, we finish off the scene by adding yummy leaves for Jenny to munch on! Use a black marker to outline any part of your painting you want to make stand out.

Perry the Puffin

Birds come in all shapes and sizes, and undoubtedly you will find rocks that will inspire you to paint some. A puffin is a fun choice because their markings are not difficult to reproduce on a rock.

1 Find a rock that is kind of egg-shaped, narrower at the top than at the bottom. Clean it with soap and water, and when it is dry, coat it with gesso or white paint.

2 We used a cream color for the main body. Mix a small amount of yellow into white and once you have a color you are happy with, paint a coat over the entire rock.

3 Add in the puffin's dark markings around the head and the body. Rather than using black, we mixed a dark purple color using blue and red.

4 The beak and feet are added using orange. The feet come up from under the body, and the beak is painted into the turn of his head.

5 We used the end of a paintbrush to dot in the eye with black, and then, with a toothpick, pulled out two eyelashes from the eye. After this has dried, a small dot of white was added as a highlight to the eye.

6 A bit more red was added to the orange color we created for the beak and feet. This darker orange was used on the beak and feet as accents. Once dry, we painted over Perry with acrylic gel to seal on the paint, and now he is ready to hit the ocean to look for a fish!

Pebble People

Have fun painting some friends for me to hang out with!

Let's start painting a face!

These charming faces are so fun to make that you will want to create your own collection! The faces are inspired by the shape of each rock. The breaks, bumps and chips in the rocks help to give each face their own unique character.

1 Select a number of similar-sized, round rocks. Wash, dry and paint with gesso.

2 Mix a skin tone color by using a tiny bit of red, some yellow and a lot of white paint. Adding in a touch of brown will make a darker tone.

3 Paint all of the rocks with the skin tone you want and let dry.

TIP: Look at each rock and see if there is anything unique to help you design the face. A broken area can become the mouth, or a bump in the rock can inspire a cool hair style, a hat or an accessory.

Tiny Tina

Tina is a cute, happy girl with little pigtails on the side of her head.

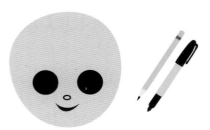

1 Choose a facial expression and use a pencil to draw the the features onto the rock. With a fine-tip marker, color in the eyes, nose and mouth.

2 Use white to carefully paint in the eyes. Two white dots in the iris create the highlights. Next, paint in eyebrows and eyelashes.

3 Mixing a bit more red into the skin tone creates a nice rosy color to paint in lips and cheeks.

4 We used two small black pompoms for Tina's pigtails. Paint the hair on first and let it dry. Then glue the pompoms on using tacky glue. Of course you can use any color you like!

5 You can add a little gemstone, sequin or other embellishment for Tina's hair. We also used a light purple shade of paint and a fine brush to add some highlights to her hair. Wrap the two pigtails with bits of colored yarn for a pretty look. Once everything is on and dried, use acrylic gel to coat the whole stone.

Lazy Larry

Be creative and make faces to express how you are feeling! Lazy Larry clearly needs to get some sleep. We used a fine tip marker to outline his features. Make some funky hair by cutting a large pom pom in half and gluing it on to the top of his head. Squish it into the shape you want.

Wailing William

The chip in this rock looked like a wide-opened mouth, so of course we painted William wailing! Use a black marker to draw on the detail, and a pipe cleaner makes a quirky hat.

Lovely Linda

A pipe cleaner hat and yarn hair are the perfect accessories for this lovely lady!

Hungry Hank

Here, the shape of the stone inspired Hungry Hank's slicked back hair. Have fun coming up with silly expressions for your pebble people!

Mini Maria

Once Maria's features were painted on, we glammed up her hair with pretty beaded accessories, glued on with tacky glue.

Green Gary

A fun and silly hairstyle was added by gluing beads on a green painted background. Try gluing on sequins, sand or sawdust for lots of other fun looks!

Seashore Stones

Mermaid

Rock painting doesn't always have to be about turning the rock into something new. Rocks can be a fun canvas simply for painting on. Here we have painted a pretty mermaid and some colorful starfish onto plain rocks. They would look lovely in a flower bed or by a pool!

1 Find a rock that you can envision a mermaid perched on. Mermaids will often sit on rocks out in the ocean to catch the sun!

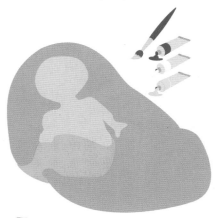

2 Sketch the outline of the mermaid onto the rock with a pencil, and then fill in the shape of her body with a light pink skin tone. Her tail was added wtih orange.

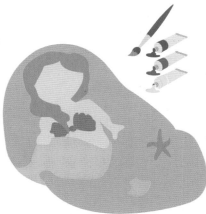

3 We mixed a lavender color with red, blue and white. Use this color to paint in her hair and bikini top. Add in a starfish and shell using the colors you have created.

4 Start to paint in detail for the scales on her tail, as well as some of the shell detail and highlights in her hair. Use some of the lavender and orange colors in the detail as well to create depth.

5 Use your smallest brush and black paint to outline the mermaid, her hair and her bikini. Add shadows to the shell and starfish. Add in eyes and a smiling mouth.

6 Look at your whole painting and add detail as you like. Add in a green hint of seaweed to the painting to create a shadow under her tail and hand. This will make it look like she is resting on the rock. A splash of blue water against the base of the rock will make her feel at home!

TIP: *These starfish have been painted to look like they are clinging to the surface of their rock. This is accomplished by using shadows and highlights to create a sense of depth. The white highlights create areas that appear to be higher than others. Black and dark grey shadows around the arms of the starfish create areas that look like they are lower. Try to use this technique yourself when you are painting starfish onto your rocks!*

Rocky Treats

mmm...   yummy!

Pizza

Yum! Yum! Who wants to take a big bite of this delicious, cheesy pizza? Not me! This rocky treat was inspired by a wedge-shaped stone, shaped just like a pizza slice.

1 Paint your clean, dry rock with gesso or white paint. Let it dry.

2 Mix a color for the pizza crust with brown and white to create a light tan color. Paint the whole rock with this to create the base color.

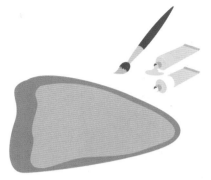

3 Cheese can be added by mixing a light yellow and then painting it all over the top of the slice. You may want to let it drip over the sides a bit, just the way a good, cheesy slice should be! Reserve some of your "cheese" to drip over the top of the ingredients you add!

4 For a pepperoni pizza, either paint the sausage on with a red paint, or use circles of red felt glued on with tacky glue.

5 Little round circles of black paper with a hole punched in the middle of them work well for olives. Again, they can be painted on as well with black paint.

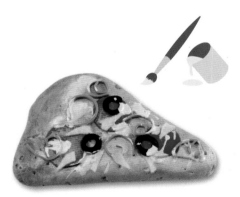

6 Depending what you like on your pizza, be creative! Pepper strips can be made from felt or paper, you can also use little bits of modelling clay if you have some at home to make all sorts of pizza toppings. Delish!

corn on the cob

1 Corn on the cob is long and cylindrical. Find a rock that is this shape, and once it is clean and dry, paint it with gesso or white paint.

2 Use a light brown to paint the base color. This will show through behind the kernels of corn.

3 Use green to paint the husk, or leaves of the corn. They normally are long and cover the whole cob until you peel them back.

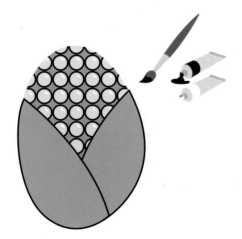

4 Paint the kernels of corn with a fresh, bright yellow.

5 Each kernel of corn should have a shadow and a highlight to make them look real. Paint all the highlights in white, on the top left corner of each kernel. Outline each kernel in dark brown to create a shadow.

6 Use a dark green to paint in details on the husks. The leaves overlap, so outline the edges in dark brown or with a fine marker first, and then add in the details of the leaves.

Strawberries

1 Fresh, sweet strawberries are delicious in the summer! Berries are usually broader at the top and taper to the bottom. See if you can find a whole little basket of stones so that you can share them with family and friends! Once they are clean and dry, paint them with gesso or white paint.

2 Of course strawberries are red, so go ahead and paint all your berries a bright, juicy red!

3 Add the leaves and stem to the top of each berry in a light green.

4 Paint on the seeds with black. Strawberry seeds are quite tiny, so you may find using a toothpick or the tip of your brush handle will work well for making the dots.

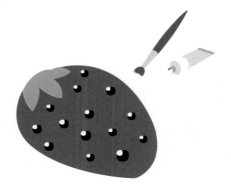

5 Once the seeds are dry, add a white highlight with a toothpick to each of the seeds. Try to place the highlight in the same spot on each of the seeds for a more realistic look.

6 Use green and yellow tones to add further detail to the leaves and stem of the berries. Enjoy!

Rock Cars

ROCK AUTO

A Rockin' Beetle

The Flintstones never had cars as fancy as these ones! For anyone who loves drawing cars, painting them on rocks is a great way to see them come to life in 3D.

1 In this case, we want the rock to be the base color as the car will be actually "driving" on the rock. So just paint on the body of the car using a light green. You may need to paint 2 or 3 coats in order to get a nice, even color.

2 Add on the tires in black.

3 The windows are painted with a light blue, which you can mix with a darker blue and white. Paint on a front windshield, a back window, and the two side windows.

4 Use a dark green to add in shape details. For example, add in the front and rear bumpers, the panels over the tires, the doors and hood of the car.

5 Create a dark gray by mixing black and white Use it to add highlights to the tires, and to outline the windows and underside of the car.

6 Use a fine brush to add white highlights to the windows, a handle on the door, front headlights, rear tail lights, a license plate, and any other details you think your car needs before you can take it on the road!

More Jungle Fun

Pudgy Panda

These animals featured here are a bit more advanced, but are well worth the effort for the beautiful results! One of the favorite animals to paint is the cute, cuddly panda. He is chubby and happy and lends himself well to rock painting.

1 Clean and dry a large, egg-shaped rock, and cover it with a layer of gesso.

2 Add a white base coat and let it dry. Lightly sketch on the arms and legs of the panda with a pencil.

3 Using black, paint in the arms and legs you just sketched, and let it dry.

4 Fill in the ears, eyes and nose of the panda using black paint and a fine brush.

5 Use a fine brush to carefully paint in the white highlights on the eyes and add some shading around the arms, legs and nose.

6 To create the feathery texture of fur, put a tiny bit of black paint on your brush, and then flatten the bristles out. With the bristles flattened out, carefully brush lightly from the arm outwards. You may want to practice this technique on a piece of paper before you try it on your panda.

Bella Peacock

Bella Peacock is a pretty animal to paint on a rock. Her colors are rich and vibrant, and creating all her feathers is fun!

1 Start by selecting a rock that is generally oval in shape. Paint it with gesso or white paint and let it dry.

2 Peacocks are shades of blue and turquoise, so choose a rich blue as the base color and paint the entire rock.

3 Once it is dry, sketch on the head and neck of the peacock and paint it in with a lighter blue color. Start to add in the "eyes" of the feather designs.

4 Add black to your blue to create a darker shade and add in eyes, feathers at the top of the head, and the area where the tail feathers are. Add in markings to each of the eyes of the feathers.

5 Use black to paint in the pupil of the eye and a few feather details. Add white highlights to the feathers on the head and the pupil. Finally paint in the white beak.

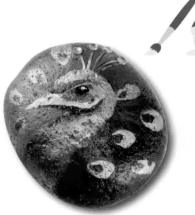

6 At this point, you can add in additional color and detail to your peacock. Or, you can use gemstones to embellish the head feathers, and sequins or glitter to add sparkle to the tail feathers. Coat the entire rock with acrylic gel to seal it.

Hootie owl

Hootie Owl stares seriously at you out of big, golden eyes. Perched on your bedroom window sill, you know he will be watching over you during the night!

1 For this fluffy little owl, use a natural stone color as the base. You want it to show through and provide some depth to the colors of his feathers. Paint over the stone in brown, not worrying if you don't cover it completely.

2 Paint in a white patch for his chest feathers. It should be kind of rough looking. Flattening your brush bristles out and not loading on very much paint will help you create a feathery effect.

3 We used different shades of brownish-orange to create other feathers. You can do this by starting with brown, and adding a bit of yellow, orange, or a little white to achieve different colors.

4 Here we are adding a bit of yellow to create interesting feathers, as well as to make his big, glowing eyes.

5 The beak and eye detail is added in a dark brown.

6 To make Hootie Owl look fluffy, randomly dab paint onto his body, with a fairly dry brush. Don't put lots of paint on your brush, just a bit, and then kind of splotch it on. Add darker and lighter colors to create the look of the feathers. Seal the rock with varnish or acrylic gel if you are using it.

Rock Age

Baby Dinosaur

Dinosaurs Rock! And for sure, when you are out looking for rocks to paint, you are going to find some that are lumpy, knobby, and chunky - perfect for a prehistoric pet! Start with this first project, the Baby Dinosaur, before moving on to one of the more complicated projects.

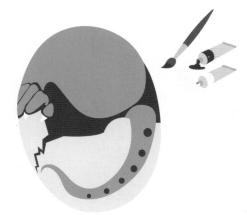

1 Paint the entire rock off-white to create the base color for the egg.

2 Use a pencil to sketch in the shape of the baby dino breaking out of his shell. Draw in the egg shell cracking as he tries to escape. Use a light green to paint in the base color for the dinosaur.

3 Add some shadow with a dark green to define his head, and add in detail on his tail and claws.

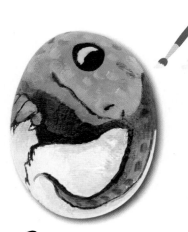

4 Use black and a fine brush to create the shadow of the egg shell, and to outline his tail, claws, and facial features.

5 Add eye detail and cheeks. At this point, take a look at the overall project and see what you would like to do to give your dinosaur some personality and detail.

6 You could add spots in lighter and darker colors, different types of markings, or anything that will make your baby dinosaur interesting!

Rockquarium

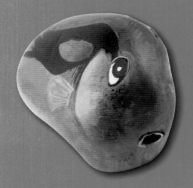

These are only a few of thousands of variations of tropical fish you can paint. If you look online at all the beautiful colors they come in, you will surely be inspired to try others!

Clown Fish

Fish come in all sorts of beautiful colors and shapes, which make them ideal for painting onto rocks. Metallic paints are perfect for replicating the shiny scales on fish, so try experimenting with some of the specialty paints that you can find in a craft store. Here we demonstrate a few of our favorite fish.

1 Clown Fish are popular and fun to paint! Their orange and white markings are very distinct, and they always have a happy face. Start by painting the base coat of gesso and let the rock dry.

2 Add a coat of bright white, and once dry, use a pencil to draw the striped markings on your Clown Fish.

3 Mix a dark orange-red color, and paint in the stripes and face of your fish. Add in a small side fin at the side of its face. Use a dry brush to do this, with the bristles spread out a bit to create a feathery look.

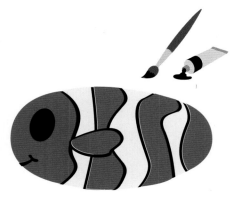

4 Use a fine brush and black paint to outline the markings and fin, as well as to create the big eyes and smiling face.

5 Add in white details for the eyes.

6 Finish your fish with 2 or 3 coats of varnish or acrylic gel to give him a bright, shiny finish, and protect him from damage.

Parrot Fish

1 A Parrot Fish has a chunky body, with a very blunt face and nose area. So find a rock that you feel will work for this fish, and once it is clean, give it a coat of gesso or white paint.

2 Establish the base color of the fish; in this case we chose a bright, emerald green. Paint the entire rock this color and let it dry.

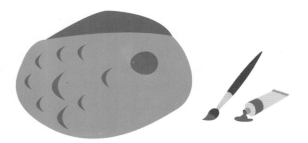

3 Dark green is used for the scale details which we painted on next around the back and sides of the fish, as well as an area where we will add in the eye.

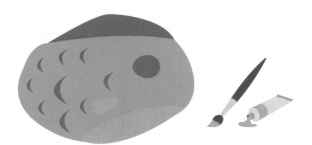

4 Tropical fish are usually warm, bright colors. For the Parrot Fish, bright yellows, greens and turquoise colors look wonderful. Paint the belly of the fish first with turquoise, and then add a darker blue fin on the side.

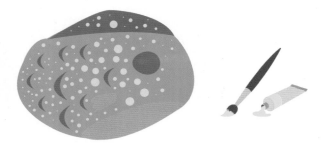

5 Parrot Fish have wild markings all over their bodies, so here we have used yellow and have painted in random dots and squiggles.

6 We have finished off our fish by using a dark blue to add detail around the mouth, the tummy and fin. Finally black is used for the eyes, and to accent the fin, and white is added as highlights.

Royal Angelfish

A Royal Angelfish is characterized by its beautiful yellow body, and striking blue and white striped markings.

1 Angelfish are a delicate and elegant fish found in tropical waters. Normally they are quite thin, so look for rocks that mimic this shape. Once you have found the right rock, clean it and prepare it with gesso or white paint.

2 The body color of a Royal Angelfish is yellow, so we have painted our rock completely with this color and let it dry.

3 Use some blue paint to show the shape of the fish's body and the base for the eye.

4 Follow the example to paint in white stripes along the body and fin area.

TIP: If you have metallic paint, mix a bit in with the yellow. This will give you a beautiful color you can use to create the look of the shiny scales of the fish's body.

5 Outline the stripes in a deep blue, and add in more eye detail. The fins are almost all blue, with only a small amount of white highlighting. Finish off your Angelfish with some white highlights on the tail and around the tummy.

Monster Madness

Rocks, Stones and Scary Things!

Making rock monsters is a lot of fun, because monsters come in all shapes and sizes, and can be created from any type of rock - the more bumpy and broken, the creepier your monster!

Here are some fun variations of monsters on these pages. Use your imagination and scraps of materials and craft supplies to inspire your own scary stones.

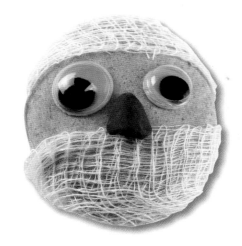

Mummy

This mummy stone was made by gluing on small pieces of gauze for the mummy wrappings. The eyes and a small stone nose were then glued on using tacky glue.

Cyclops

These monsters are more cute than they are scary! Follow these simple steps to create your own one-eyed rock creatures.

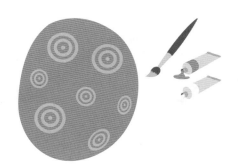

1 Coat your rock with gesso. Once it is dry, choose a base color and paint your rock in that color.

2 Use your base color to create a lighter shade by adding white, and a darker shade by adding some black. Use these colors to add swirls and dots on your monsters.

3 We cut a short length of pipe cleaner and wrapped it around a pencil to create the antenna, and then used tacky glue to attach it to the top of the monster's head. An eye was glued onto the center of the forehead to create the cyclops.

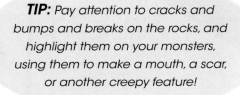

TIP: Pay attention to cracks and bumps and breaks on the rocks, and highlight them on your monsters, using them to make a mouth, a scar, or another creepy feature!

Rocky Zen Garden

Zen gardens are used to help you relax as you rake the sand into patterns around your rocks, and to help you improve concentration.

Creating a mini zen garden is simple to do, and a cool way to display some of your special rocks. The rocks can be ones you have found while on vacation, or that have special meaning to you. If you have painted some rocks that you want to show off, this is a great way to do it.

To make your own zen garden, fill a shoe box lid or a shallow, rectangular pan with sand. Place your rocks into the sand in a decorative way. You could select one large one as the focus, and group a few smaller pebbles around it. Using a plastic fork that you have trimmed down to act as a little rake, rake the sand around your rocks, creating wave patterns in the sand.

As you are studying the patterns you are creating in the sand around your rocks, use the time to think about a problem and how to solve it, or to meditate and achieve calmness!

Five Stones

This game is an entertaining, competitive game that requires some hand - eye skills and great timing. It is played in rounds.

How to Play:

Round 1

Throw 5 stones into the air with one hand, and try to catch as many as possible on the back of that same hand.

Flick the stones off the back of your hand, into the air again and then try to catch them in the palm of your hand.

If you don't have any stones in your hand at this point, then your turn is over and it is the other players turn. Repeat this round until you succeed in catching at least one remaining stone.

Round 2

Keep one stone in your hand, and toss the remaining stones on the ground. Toss the stone in your hand into the air. While it is in the air, pick up one stone from the ground and then catch the stone you tossed - all with the same hand.

Toss the two stones into the air, pick up the next stone from the ground, and catch the two stones from the air.

Continue until you have picked up all the stones from the ground.

Round 3

Keep one stone in your hand, toss the remaining four on the ground and then try to pick them up two at a time.

Round 4

Keep one stone in your hand and then try to pick up 3 stones at once, and then the remaining stone.

Round 5

Keep one stone in your hand and then try to pick up all four stones at once.

Additional Challenge

If you would like to continue playing, you can repeat these five rounds, but add in a challenge. The challenge could be:

Clap your hands once before you catch the stone.

Spin around before you catch the stone.

Slap your knees before you catch the stone.

And so on...

The Perfect Stones

Make your own set of custom stones for this game. Paint them special colors, add numbers, or create a design that you feel will bring you luck. Make sure you coat your stones with 2 or 3 layers of acrylic gel and let them dry thoroughly to protect them and keep them from chipping.

Hopscotch

Hopscotch is a fun game to play outside; it dates back to Roman times and used to be played by the soldiers who would see how far they could jump carrying weights! Today, it is much less exhausting to play, but still requires a level of skill that you will gain as you practice with your friends.

make your own hopscotch stone

A hopscotch stone needs to be one you can throw easily to the end of the board. It can't be too heavy to throw, but it can't be so light that it bounces after you throw it. A flat stone works better than a round one, because you don't want it to roll after it lands.

Once you have found the perfect stone, paint it with your lucky design, and coat it with 2 or 3 layers of acrylic gel, so that your design won't chip away when it is in play.

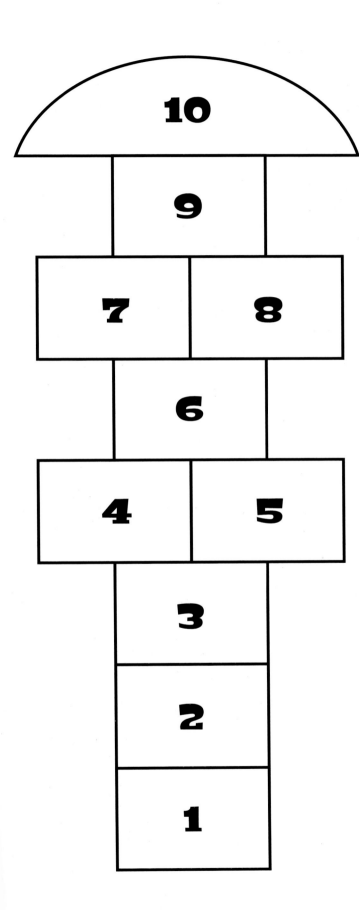

Here is how you play:

With a piece of sidewalk chalk, draw a hopscotch board into the ground - one that looks like the diagram. There should be 10 sections, each with a number in them.

Stand behind the start line, and using your special hopscotch stone, toss it into square 1.

Stand on one leg and hop over square 1, into square 2 and then into square 3.

Use both feet to hop into squares 4 and 5 - one foot should land in each square.

Hop into square 6 on one leg, then with both feet into square 7 and 8.

Hop into square 9 on one leg, and then both feet into square 10.

Turn around and hop back through the grid in the same way you went through it. Stop on square 2, and without putting your other foot down or touching the ground with your hand, bend over and pick up your rock from square 1. Hop into square 1 and then back over the finish line.

If you successfully hop the grid, then you can toss your stone into square 2. Continue playing as long as you can until you break one of the rules. If you break one of the rules, then put your marker into the corner of the square that you didn't successfully complete so that you can remember where to start the next round.

Once your turn is over, it passes to the next player. The first person to complete the full grid to 10 wins.

Don't forget the rules!

• You must hop over the square where the marker has landed, without touching any part of that square.

• You can't step on any of the lines, land in the wrong square, or touch your other foot down if you are outside of the double squares.

• Don't lose your balance when you are bending down to pick up your rock on the way back.

Astrological Stones

Do you know your sign? Depending on when you were born, you will have a specific star sign, and some of the qualities associated with that sign. A star sign stone would make a super cute gift for a friend on their birthday!

Pisces:
Mysterious, adaptable & talented
The sign of Pisces is the fish
February 19 - March 20

Aquarius:
Trend-setter, leader & intelligent
The sign of Aquarius is water
January 20 - Feburary 18

Aries:
Adventurous, active & outgoing
The sign of Aries is a ram
March 21 - April 19

Gemini:
Curious, talkative & intelligent
The sign of Gemini is the twins
May 21 - June 20

Taurus:
Calm, determined & reserved
The sign of Taurus is the bull
April 20 - May 20

Cancer:
Mysterious, interesting & caring
The sign of Cancer is the crab
June 21 - July 22

Leo:
Lucky, faithful & positive
The sign of Leo is the lion
July 23 - August 22

Virgo:
Creative, sensitive & giving
The sign of Virgo is a young lady
August 23 - September 22

Libra:
Charming, creative & friendly
The sign of Libra is the scales
September 23 - October 22

Scorpio:
Wise, powerful & dramatic
The sign of Scorpio is a scorpion
October 23 - November 21

Sagittarius:
Optimistic, honest & free-spirited
The symbol of Sagittarius is the archer
November 22 - December 21

Capricorn:
Ambitious, patient & persevering
The symbol of Capricorn is the goat
December 22 - January 19

More creative ideas... think about special holidays like
Christmas, Halloween or Easter and paint, paint, Paint!
The important thing is to have fun being creative.

About the Artists

Danny Han-Lin Chen and Hilda Yuet Yi Chen are artists and instructors from Richmond, BC, Canada. Aside from their classes in contemporary Chinese Brush painting, acrylic, mixed media and watercolor, they now offer rock painting workshops to people of all ages. Danny has been featured in the *International Artist* magazine, and has received many awards and recognitions in world-class art competitions for his work. A popular painting instructor with over 35 years teaching experience, Danny is known for his diversity of knowledge about art, and his compassionate approach to painting and creating.

Hilda received her degree in Design & Communication from RMIT in Australia, and loves to work with acrylics and mixed media. She is particularly passionate about painting portraits and in capturing the spirit and characters of children. Hilda is an adventurous artist and constantly is learning new techniques and searching for new inspiration.

Rock painting is an excellent craft for young children, teaching them about about observation and imagination, and it is a hobby Danny and Hilda have been developing since their daughter Jasmine was born. Taking walks on the beach to look for different rocks to paint is a favorite evening activity, and even at the age of 3, she is able to participate in choosing the rocks, cleaning them, and painting them with gesso. Jasmine is learning to paint simple subjects such as flowers and frogs. Her favorite projects in this book were the bunny and chicken magnet!

For more information, please visit:
www.chensgallery.com

Meet the Violin

scroll

Tuning Peg

Finger Board

shoulder

Ribs

F Hole

Tail Piece

Chin Rest

Bow tip

stick

Hair

Bridge

Frog

screw

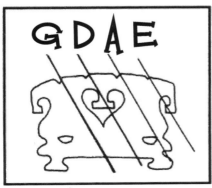

G D A E

Play-a-long mp3 accompaniments are available on the website at:
www.musicfunbooks.com/vfb

Also available is the piano accompaniment book.
The Violin Fun Book Piano Accompaniment
(ISBN#1091831114 *or* 978-1091831117)

Viola, cello and bass books are also available.

Take online violin lessons using The Violin Fun Book.
Register at **www.musicfunbooks.com/lessons**

2

Welcome to the wonderful world of violin!

Let's begin with plucking!

My First Song

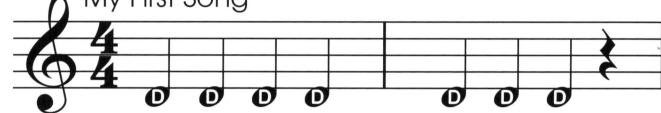

Notes and Rests

Three's a Crowd

Getting Tricky

4

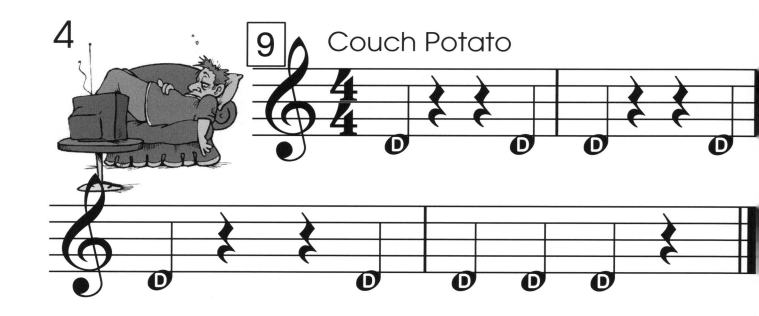

Couch Potato

Meet the "A" Team

Puppy Dog Song

Eyes on the Road

6

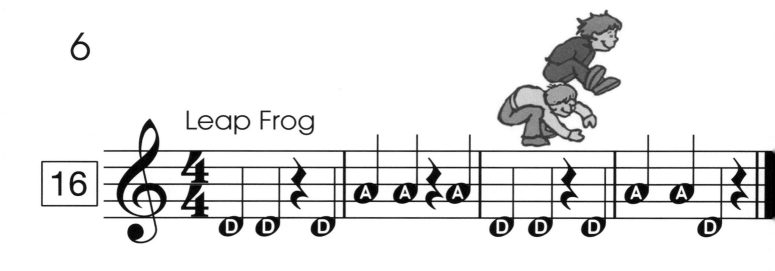

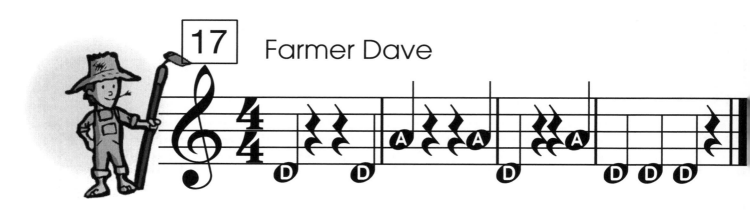

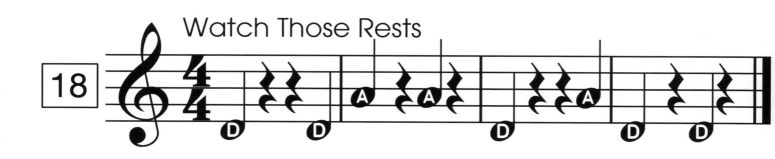

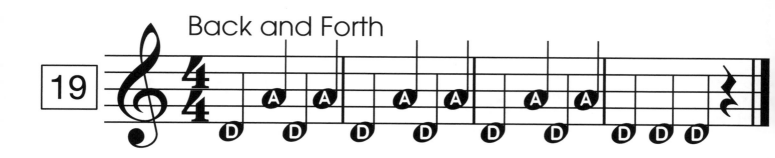

Learning the Bow Grip

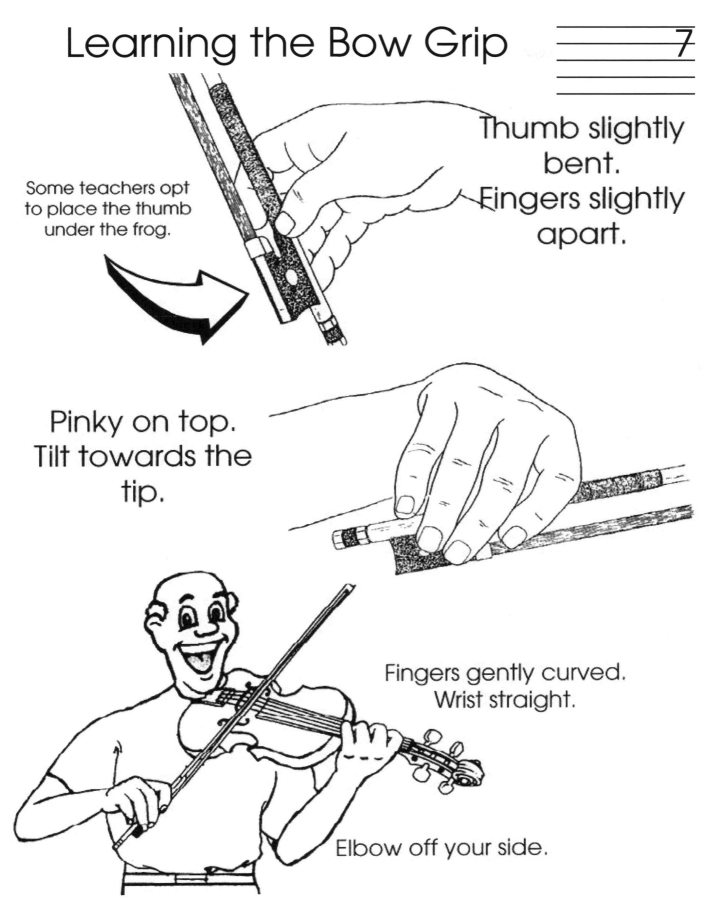

Some teachers opt to place the thumb under the frog.

Thumb slightly bent.
Fingers slightly apart.

Pinky on top.
Tilt towards the tip.

Fingers gently curved.
Wrist straight.

Elbow off your side.

Now go back and play the first part of the book again with the bow.

First Finger "E"

NEW NOTE

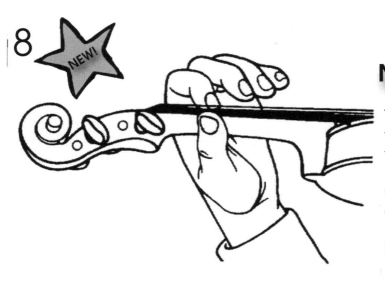

To play our new note, place the first finger of your left hand down on the "D" string's first tape or mark.

Curve your fingers & use the tip of of your pointer finger on the "D" string

Relax your thumb.

Press firmly and play the "D" string with your bow.

My First Finger E
20

The Fabulous Mr. Ed
21

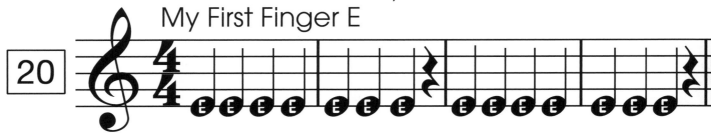

Fun with D and E
22

Banana Split
23

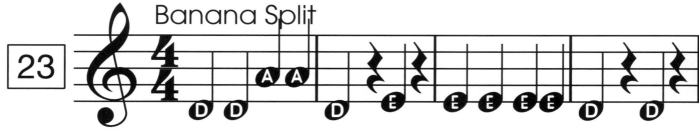

Second Finger 9
"F#"

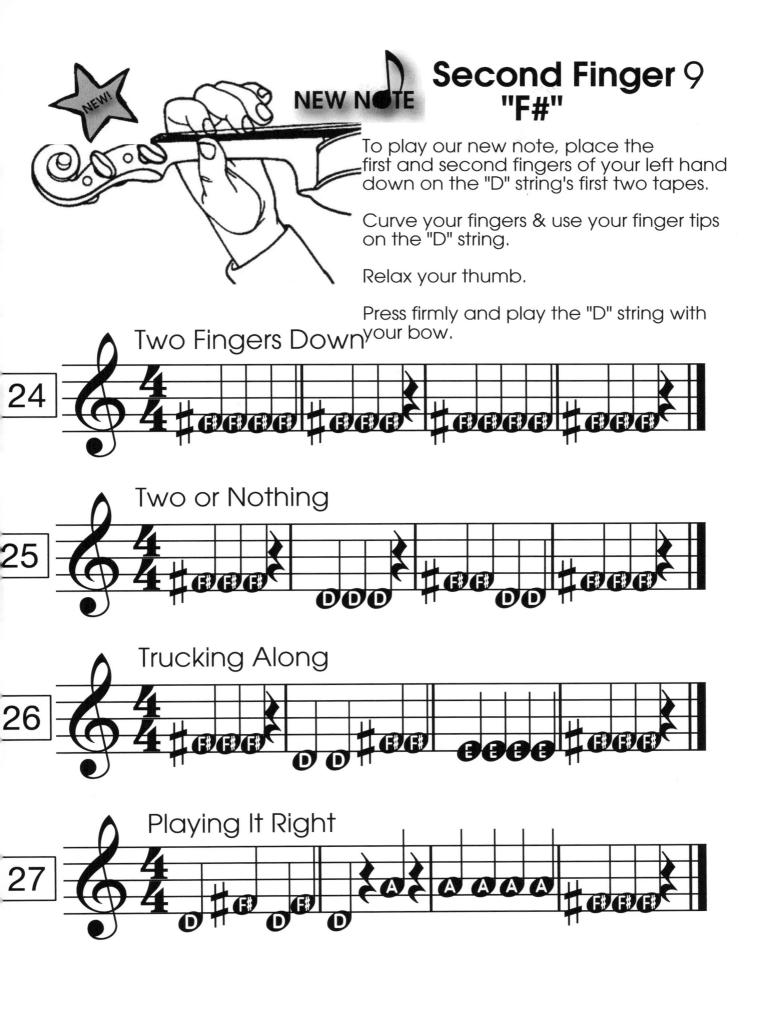

NEW NOTE

To play our new note, place the first and second fingers of your left hand down on the "D" string's first two tapes.

Curve your fingers & use your finger tips on the "D" string.

Relax your thumb.

Press firmly and play the "D" string with your bow.

Two Fingers Down

24

Two or Nothing

25

Trucking Along

26

Playing It Right

27

Quarter notes get one beat of sound.

Whole notes get four beats of sound.

Quarter note rests get one beat of silence.

♩ **Half Note**

Two Beats of Sound

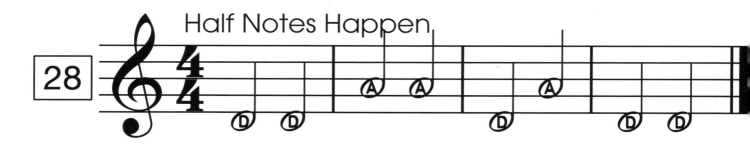

28 — Half Notes Happen

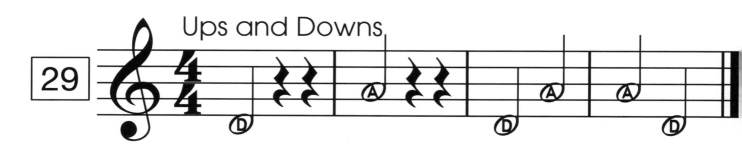

29 — Ups and Downs

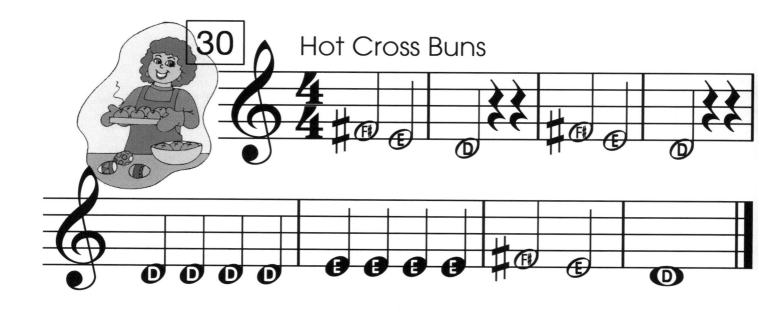

30 — Hot Cross Buns

Time Signature

When you see this time signature,
you have four beats in each measure.

31 Mary Had A Little Lamb

32 French Fries

33 Karate Chop

34 Soccer Champ

Winning the Prize

35

14

The Ballerinas

36

The Boy Scout

37

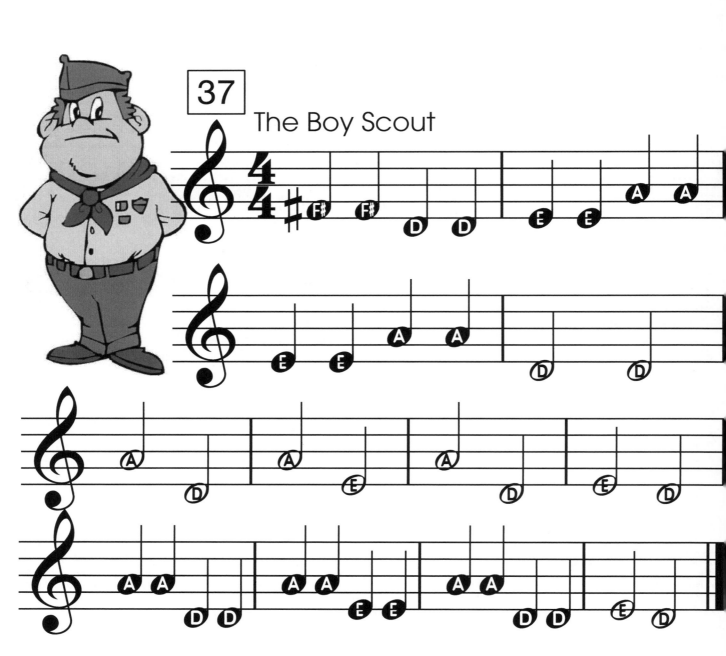

16

Lightly Row

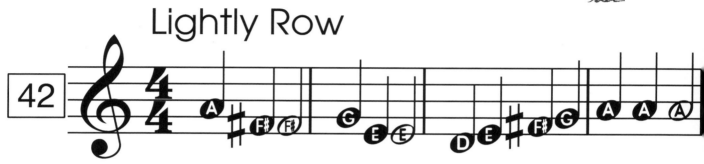

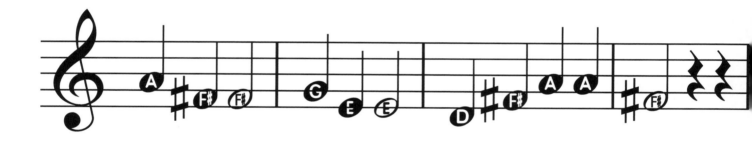

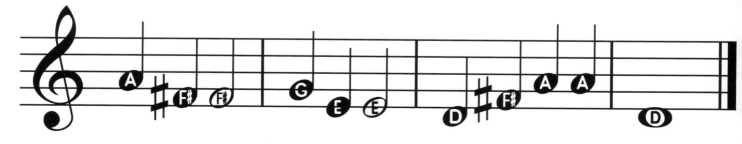

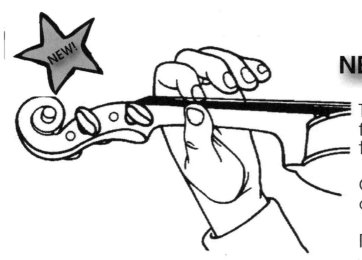

"B"

To play our new note, place the first finger of your left hand down on the "A" string's first tape or mark.

Curve your fingers & use the tip of of your pointer finger on the "A" string.

Relax your thumb.

Press firmly and play the "A" string with your bow.

Better "B" Good

"A" vs. "B"

Song Without Letters

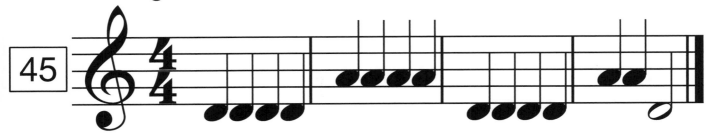

18

Twinkle, Twinkle, Little Star

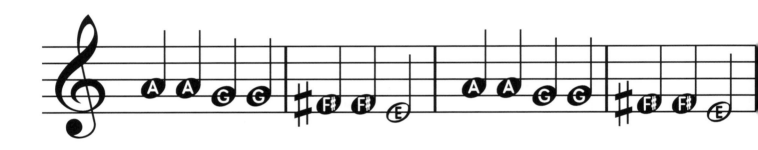

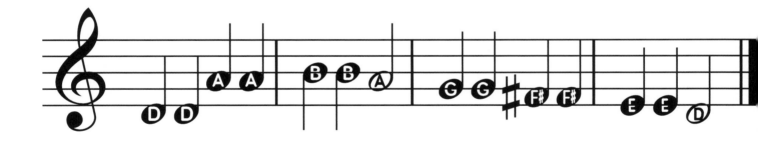

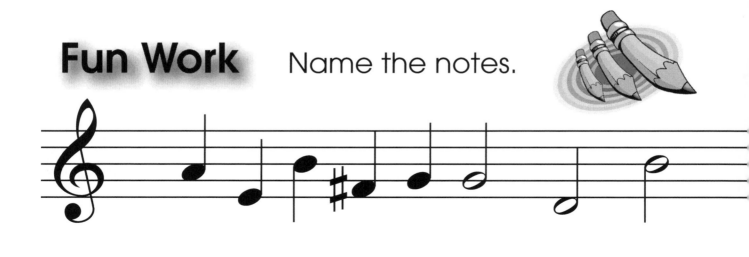

Fun Work   Name the notes.

DOWN BOW

Move the bow away from your body (to the right) for a DOWN bow.

∨

UP BOW

Move the bow toward your body (to the left) for an UP bow.

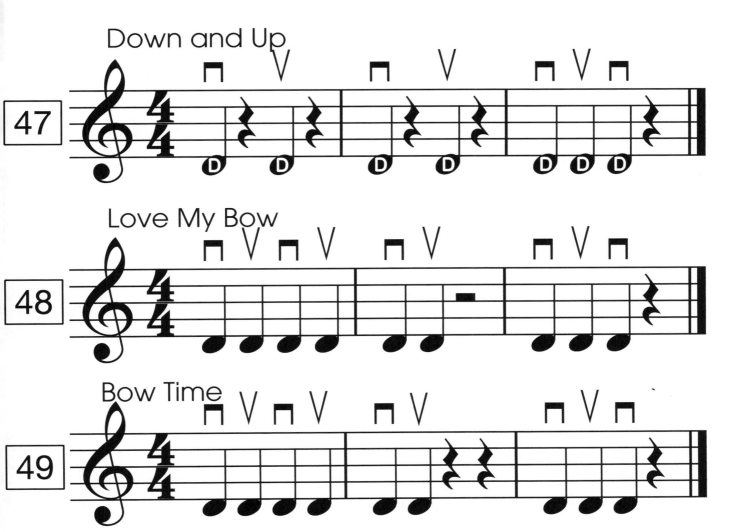

Down and Up

47

Love My Bow

48

Bow Time

49

20

LIFT

When you come to a comma, LIFT and start with a new bow.

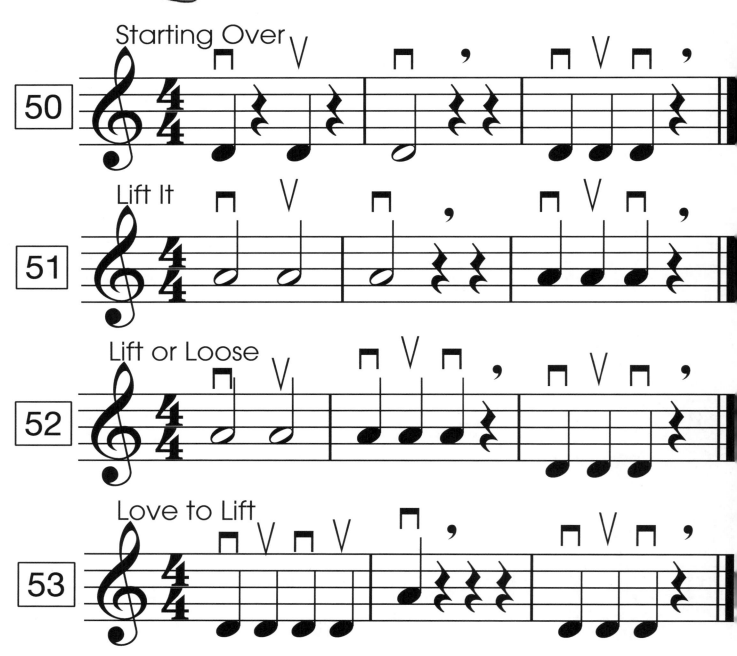

Starting Over

50

Lift It

51

Lift or Loose

52

Love to Lift

53

Jingle Bells

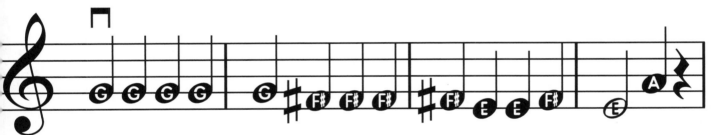

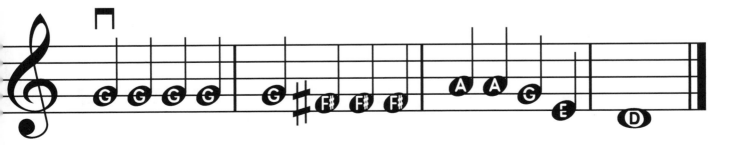

London Bridge

56

A dotted half note gets three beats of sound.

Three Counts Each

57

Careful Counter

58

24

59 Hey, Diddle, Diddle

60 Cukoo Bird

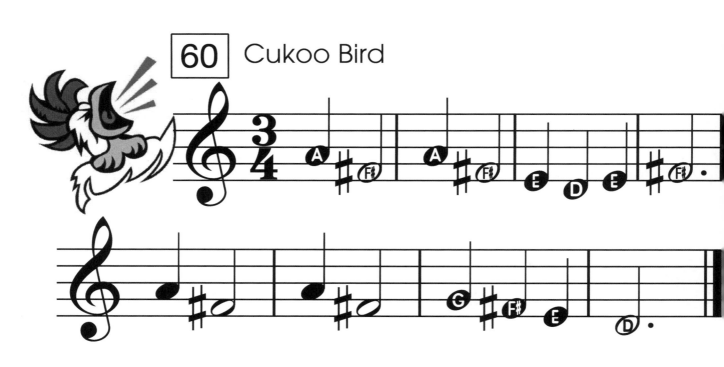

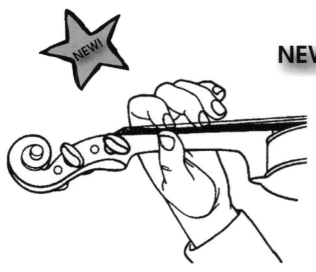

NEW NOTE "C#"

To play our new note, place the first and second fingers of your left hand down on the "A" string's first two tapes.

Curve your fingers & use your finger tips on the "A" string.

Relax your thumb.

Press firmly and play the "A" string with your bow.

I See "C" Sharp

Hot Cross Buns on the "A" String

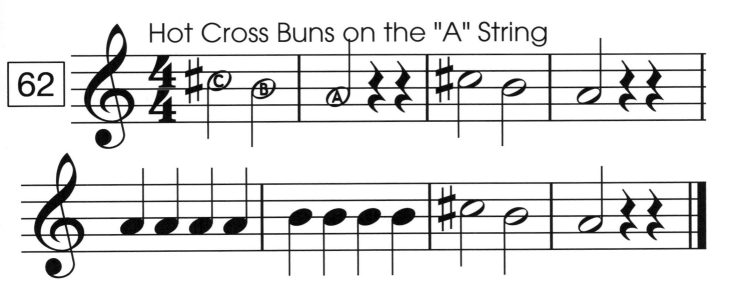

Climbing Up and Down

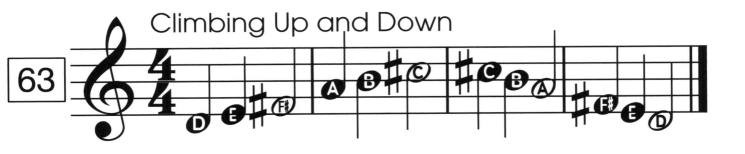

Jump Right In

64

We Can All Read!

65

Fun Work

Name the notes written on the staff below.

Third Finger 27
"D"

NEW NOTE

To play our new note, place the first, second and third fingers of your left hand down on the "A" string's first three tapes.

Curve your fingers & use your finger tips on the "A" string.

Relax your thumb.

Press firmly and play the "D" string with your bow.

Meet the Mr. "D"

66

My Sombrero

67

The Eagle Waltz

68

Pencil and Eraser Waltz

69

Buffalo Gals

70

Tie

A "tie" is a curved line that connects two or more notes of the same pitch.

Hold the note for the combined value of the notes.

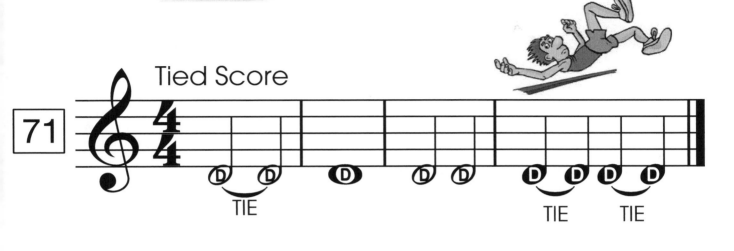

Tied Score

71

TIE   **TIE**   **TIE**

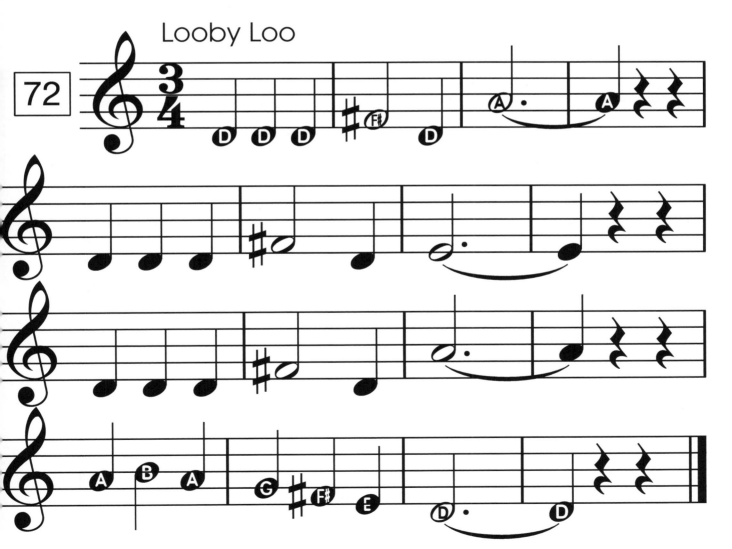

Looby Loo

72

30

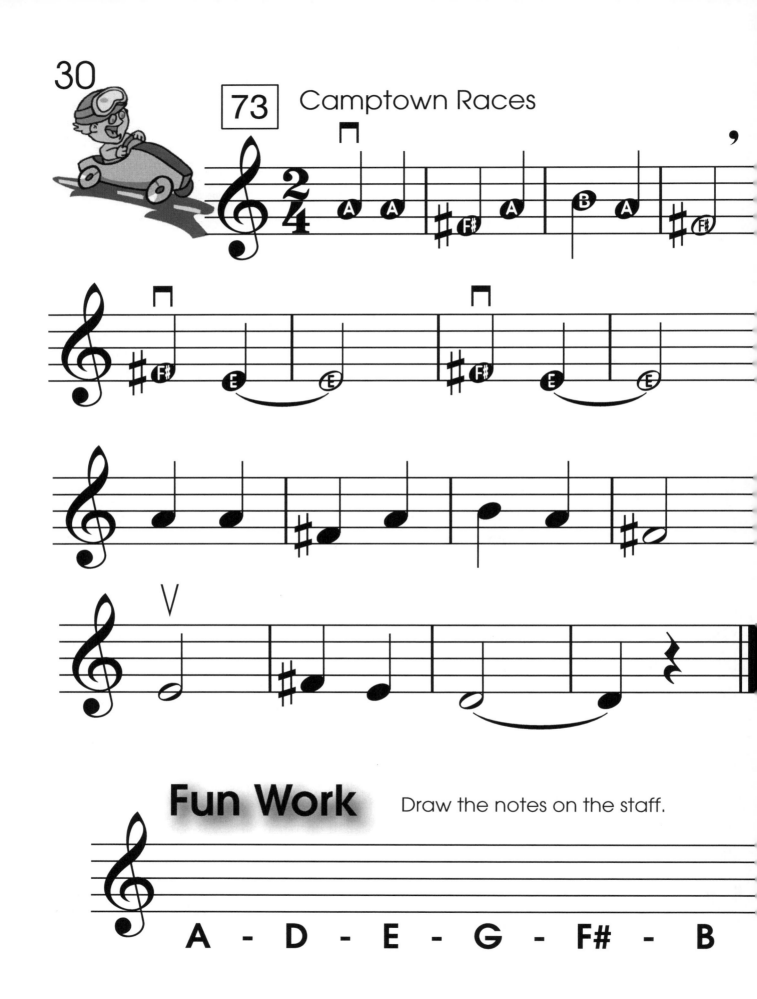

Fun Work Draw the notes on the staff.

A - D - E - G - F# - B

To play our new note, raise your right elbow slightly and play your open "G" string (fattest string).

Open "G" is below the music staff.

It is the lowest sounding note on the violin.

NEW NOTE 31

My Low, Fat "G"

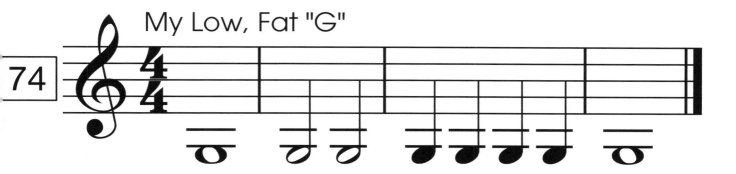

74

Grandma's Tune

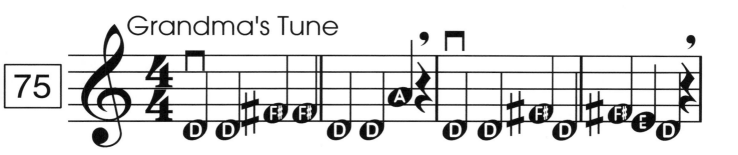

75

Oh Susannah

Eigth Notes

One eighth note gets 1/2 count.
Two eighth notes get ONE count.

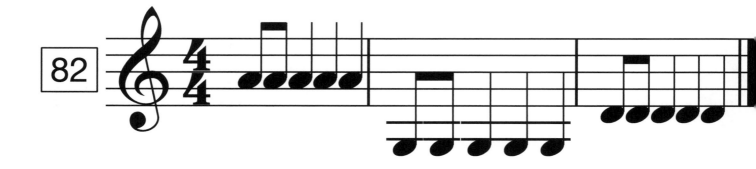

Dynamics

_p_ Piano
Play with a soft volume.

_f_ Forte
Play with a loud volume.

Key Signature

When you see two sharps at the beginning of a song, play all the F and C notes as sharp notes.

Cabbage Song

83

Humpty Dumpty

84

Slur

A SLUR is a curved line that connects two notes of different pitches.

Move you bow in the same direction for the slurred notes. Don't stop the bow. Use an equal amount of bow for each note in the slur.

38

87 Clowns of Paris

88 Ode to Joy

Good King Wenceslas

Aura Lee

Frog Song

41

Dreydl, Dreydl

Jolly Old St. Nicholas

42

The Bridge at Avignon

Pop Goes the Weasel

Are You Sleeping?

Musette

44

Lo Yisa Goy

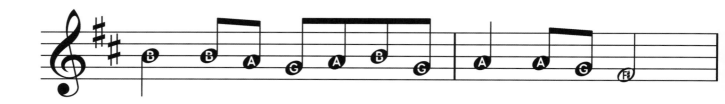
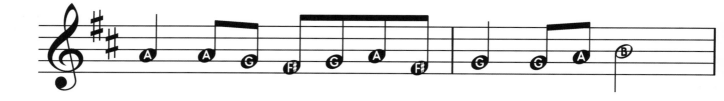

Symphony No.1 by Brahms

This Little Light of Mine

Largo from New World Symphony

47

Kum Ba Yah

Shepherd's Hey

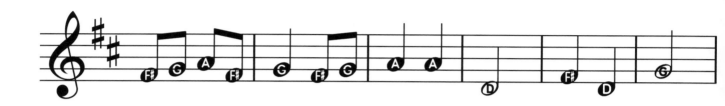

Name the Parts

Name the Strings

Matching Game

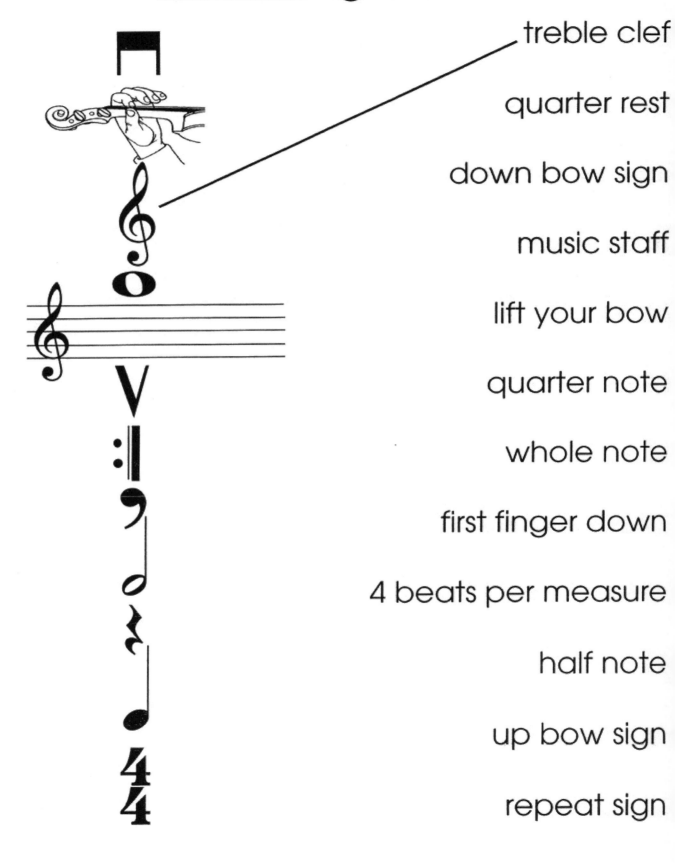

treble clef

quarter rest

down bow sign

music staff

lift your bow

quarter note

whole note

first finger down

4 beats per measure

half note

up bow sign

repeat sign

Fun Work

Write in the letters to these notes.

Notes on the D string only.

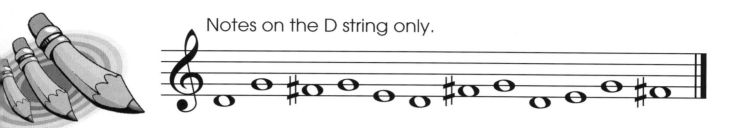

Notes on the A string only.

Notes on the G string, D string and A strings.

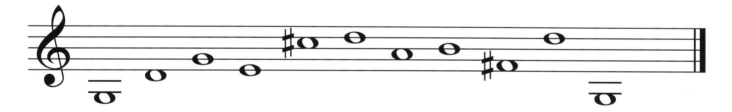

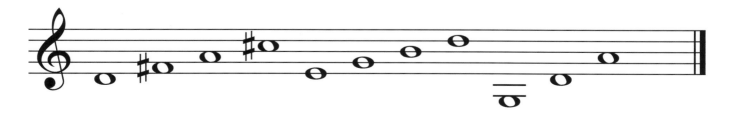

Violin

Y is for Violin

Violin

Violin

Cello

Bass

Flute

saxophone

Trumpet

French Horn

Trombone

Tuba

Congos

Guitar

Piano

Made in the USA
Middletown, DE
27 October 2021